Sacred Reciprocity

Courting *the* Beloved *in* Everyday Life

Also by Jamie K. Reaser for Hiraeth Press:

Note to Self:
Poems for Changing the World from the Inside Out

Huntley Meadows:
A Naturalist's Journal in Verse

Courting the Wild:
Love Affairs with Reptiles and Amphibians

with Susan Chernak McElroy

Courting the Wild:
Love Affairs with the Land

Sacred Reciprocity

Courting *the* Beloved *in* Everyday Life

Jamie K. Reaser

HIRAETH PRESS
DANVERS MASSACHUSETTS

Copyright © 2012 by Jamie K. Reaser

All Rights Reserved. This book may not be reproduced, in whole or in part, stored in a retrieval system, or transmitted in any form or by any means without permission from the publisher, except by a reviewer who may quote brief passages.

For information or permissions write:
Hiraeth Press, PO Box 1442
Pawcatuck, Connecticut 06379

FIRST EDITION

ISBN: 978-0-9835852-8-2

VISIT HIRAETH PRESS:
WWW.HIRAETHPRESS.COM

BOOK DESIGN
Front Cover Image © Jamie K. Reaser
Author Image by Paul Goosens
Interior Design by Leslie M. Browning and Jason Kirkey
Cover Design by Jason Kirkey and Jamie K. Reaser

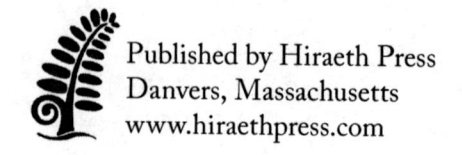

Published by Hiraeth Press
Danvers, Massachusetts
www.hiraethpress.com

For the Beloved,
and all those who court the Beloved

The Poet's Eyes

To see the world
through soft eyes
is to See the world
through the poet's eyes.

Duality blurs into Unity
when it is the heart
that manifests Vision.

'Round and 'round
the ancient dihedral
dances the Beloved's
suitor.

Surely he finds himself
liquored on his own breath
when he realizes
it is he in the spotless looking glass
gazing gently
upon the soul of the world.

Contents

vii · THE POET'S EYES
xiii · INTRODUCTION
xv · THE BELOVED

Spring

3 · A Tiny Plot of Land
5 · Daffodil
6 · Dawn Kiss
7 · Dense Mists
8 · Evidence of Life Unseen
10 · Insignificance
12 · Intimacy
15 · Irrational Optimism
17 · Lady Toad
18 · Nectar
19 · Simply Divine
21 · Storm Clouds
22 · Tadpoles in Tire Rut
23 · The Beloved's Breath
24 · The Fiddlehead Song
27 · The Indigo Bunting
28 · The Unfurling
29 · The Vittles of Death

Summer

35 · Affections
36 · Answers for Mary
37 · Berry Picking
38 · Cicadas
40 · Co-Dependency
41 · Hermit Thrushes in the Morning
43 · Sliver Moon
45 · Summer Rain
46 · The Breeze
47 · The Cattail
48 · The Insistent Moth
50 · The Nightingale
55 · The Primary Drought
57 · To Be Moved
58 · What is Joy to the Snapping Turtle?
60 · When They Make Love
61 · Wild Honey

Autumn

- 65 · A Walking Stick Sighting
- 66 · Asters Under a Hunter's Moon
- 67 · Autumnal Equinox
- 68 · Cellular Memory
- 69 · Each Sunrise
- 70 · Falling from Grace
- 71 · Fallow
- 74 · In the Dark of Night
- 75 · Pruning
- 76 · Taking a Walk
- 77 · The Directions of the Geese
- 78 · The Mud Puddle
- 79 · The Silence
- 80 · Touching

Winter

- 83 · An Answer
- 85 · Courting the Darkness
- 86 · Departing Storms
- 89 · In the Frost Crystals
- 90 · In This Way
- 93 · Sacraments
- 95 · Solstice Moon
- 96 · The Humming
- 99 · The Melting Point
- 102 · The Silent Retreat
- 104 · The Universe Unfolds
- 106 · The Winter Wren
- 108 · True Nature
- 111 · Whooo
- 114 · Resolutions

- 119 · ACKNOWLEDGEMENTS
- 121 · ABOUT THE AUTHOR

- 123 · I WISH FOR ONLY THIS

Introduction

*Tsze-Kung asked, "Is there one word which may serve
as a rule of practice for all one's life?" The Master said,
"Is not Reciprocity such a word?"* — *Confucius*

I was first introduced to the concept of 'ayni,' a Quechua word, in November of 2000 by mystic don Americo Yabar as we traversed the Andean landscape, visiting Peru's sacred sites and engaging in ceremonies that had been passed down to contemporary indigenous peoples by their Inca ancestors.

The essence of ayni is sacred reciprocity.

There is no way to directly translate or conceptualize ayni from the perspective of what has come to be known as 'western culture'; our cosmology is largely goal-oriented with a focus on tangible outcomes, while ayni emerges out of a universal perspective in which importance is placed on the relational flow of energy as a process of establishing and maintaining balance. Ayni is enacted through the energies exchanged in gifting and receiving, and it knows no bounds – ayni can be established among people, between humans and all other beings, and between all beings and the animate Cosmos.

Ayni can be seen as a code of conduct – a sacred agreement to engage in a balanced exchange between self and other. You give, I give in return. I give, you give in return. What is given may not be anywhere near as important as how it is given. In ayni, it is the heart that counts.

Sacred Reciprocity: Courting the Beloved in Everyday Life is a poetic reflection of my daily practice of embodying anyi as a core life principle. Each poem arises out of a conversation between my soul and something greater than my Self. I listen, process, reply, and begin listening again. In this book the poems themselves represent my 'give back' to Nature and the greater Cosmos for breathing life into me through tangible and intangible relationship.

I choose the word 'courting' because it describes an expressive exchange between two would-be lovers; love being the energy with the most creative potential. The word 'beloved' appears in the title and in several of the poems as a manifest of the sacred energy that unites all aspects of the universe at the Source. And, since the beloved permeates everything, it is a shapeshifter in this collection – sometimes appearing as an aspect of Self, a plant or animal or element, a notion, a heavenly body, and frequently as the Great Mystery – unknown to even the poet.

I present *Sacred Reciprocity* as an offering to you. It is an honor to pass these poems on to those who wish to receive them. May each poem carry with it an answer to a question that you have put to the universe, consciously or otherwise. May a conversation ensue. And, may the collection serve as a guide to living the principle of ayni – a guide into a deeper, richer, more balanced relationship with the universe. And, may you come to see and treat yourSelf and all others as sacred aspects of the Beloved.

—Jamie K. Reaser
Blue Ridge Mountains, Virginia

The Beloved

I have not complete knowledge
of who or what the Beloved is
for I am not complete.

Longed for by name,
the Beloved
draws near enough
to share my breath,

but the Beloved's touch
is yet too holy to grasp –

I am loved most in the
act of being forsaken
to the Great Mystery.

Truth must be a candle
without a flame
because in the spark lies
the light and the self-destruction.

Courting the Beloved
is the act of apprenticing
to the way Home.

There is no possibility
of return other than to
step upon one's own
heart –
Again and again,
until,

Broken,
the doorway
yields.

It is at this threshold
that the Beloved
recognizes
the Beloved.

In we go.

Spring

A Tiny Plot Of Land

There is a tiny plot of land I tend:
miniature daffodils,
bearded iris,
spiderwort
at the base of bluebird box
on post,
frequented by generations
of Carolina chickadees.

Thick layers of shredded cedar mulch
invite hemlocks to headstart.
It pains me to pull them.
Relocation attempts have thus far failed –
their roots run deep.
I make apologies by the season.

Sometimes I venture a few feet
forward
or backward
or to the sides
and tend tiny plots of mown grass –
pick up sticks,
brush off leaves,
offer a neighborly "hello."

But I always return
to my named plot –
sit for spell and ponder
or just sit.
Still.

Today, while planting a single-bloomed iris,
white,
vein-trimmed in deep royal purple…

Today it occurred to me that
no matter where I live
this two by three spread
will be the one plot of land that
I nurture the longest in this lifetime,
and with the most gratitude.

The blue ceramic urn below
no doubt
cracked open long ago.

It's been sixteen years.

Happy Mother's Day.

Daffodil

His yellow smock
offers no apologies
for its brazen attempt
to embody the bold cry
that we fear might pass
our own lips.

Even on culturally accepted
moments of
ecstatic inspiration –

Such as the viewing
of spring-time blooms –

So many will remain
wanton of their
expression
of Glory.

Dawn Kiss

The Sun,
dressed in dawn robes,
rose with time enough
to kiss the Moon, his beloved,
on full, wanting lips.

Birds,
still distinguishing themselves from
the wings of dreamtime,
looked abashedly at each other,
wondering...

How often had they
failed to seize
a precious passing moment...

A moment that could have
united the transiting heavens.

That was the morning birds
decided to sing.

Dense Mists

The great blue heron
tickles her breast
on springtime buds
as she
lifts and plunges
her laborious wings
over a ridgetop canopy
wet with dense mists
at dusk.

I do believe that Nature
knows something
of foreplay.

Evidence Of Life Unseen

A white-tailed buck visited pond-edge,
the light of Jupiter and new moon
dancing upon his back like giddy nymphs
at the first ball of Spring.

It was the willow sapling who told me
of his visit, the story emerging into the lines
of my palm as I ran my hand over the long,
rough, tawny wounds spanning two feet
of its narrow spine:

A rubbing post for velvet.

Time and temperature and penetrating rains
have beckoned forth spotted salamanders.
Thick as a thumb, jet black, and each marked
with a constellation like none-other,
they have crawled from their subterranean haunts
into what we call the world.

I know of this from the still-chilled waters of the vernal pool,
a receptive womb in which opaque globular egg masses float
amongst the decaying legs of last season's cattails:

Freshwater pearls encasing the bounty.
Someone trained in the arts of deep allurement,
put out a line and a bunch of foolish catfish took the bait.
He filleted them and, for reasons I cannot fathom,
drove the whiskered heads high into the mountains

where he pitched them aside in a quiet holler,
their eyes still plump with surprise.

Turkey vultures with bad breath tattled on him,
launching their heavy bodies from leafy ground to barren tree
when disturbed by the words:

"What the heck?!"

A woman sat on a rock with a purring marmalade cat,
content, watching the breeze play finger games
in his mistress' long silvery hair.
She did nothing more apparent
than write a poem.

You can see for yourself:

Everywhere there are stories being told
to eyes willing to listen.

Insignificance

I have decided to revel
in my insignificance.

I am nothing more than
anything else:

star dust,

a whisper in sacred space,

the glint in a buck's eye
during spring rut,

a mountain turned to
sand after millennia
of dying the warrior's
death,

an ant carrying cut leaf bits
back to its family
of thousands,

the dry, outgrown skin of
a black rat snake hanging
loosely in the arc of long,
wind-blown grasses.

This is all.

And in this, I am free.

My once-raucous mind has no more need
of that which does not serve
the soul's manifestation
of itSelf.

When the loyal soldier is honorably
relieved of his duties
and the long-wailing children
are nurtured,
a quietude sets in.

I walk among you having
put down my weapons
of charitlessness.

See me as nothing more than
your heart,
your prayers,
your revelation of beauty.

For, this is all I am.

I am this insignificant.

I am no better than anything
else in this exquisite
world that I wholeheartedly
share with you.

Intimacy

The morning light as it peeks in from the East,
finding me still snuggled under a duvet of
owl-winged dreams,
whispers with a lisp of hopeful eroticism,
"Are you awake?"

The barking dog beckoning as the day takes hold,

"Come, come! I have something to show you!"

And I rise, pulling on aged moccasins
and little more, following her up a rain-slick
mountain slope, brushing past ferns and
taking the piercing of brambles as love nips,
until we reach the erect truck of an old cedar tree,

and up there I see two large raccoons
making love.

The wind choreographing the boxwood boughs at
the perimeter of the old homestead,
nimble enough to remember who planted them
and why he felt so drawn to keep the
company of evergreen shrubs.

His longing for relationship grows here like an
ever-deepening caress upon the land,
like a caress upon the body.

I am touched by his handiwork, daily,
though we've never met
and chances are good that She's long since
welcomed a man like that
into Her.

The ultisol soils that occupy the garden bed
and the underlayment of my nails
on the very best of days.

Hundreds of thousands of years in the making
and molding, clay from the bodies of
the requisite dead,
feeds me each time I bring a piece
of dark, curly-leafed kale to my pale lips.

Washing is such a complex act:

It requires you to decide between lovers —
water or dirt.

Sometimes I want to let them both take hold.

You,

You permitting me see what remains wild
in your eyes, what you have refused
to give away to the hungry forces that would
domesticate your soul and talk of it
as a conceptual framework for corporate
earnings.

Oh and me,

Me surrendering to the wet touch
of this one glistening, salty tear
as it glides over my sun-danced cheek

and drops

into the abyss of neither
here nor there –

an offering of reciprocity for
the intimate communion

that awakens me.

Irrational Optimism

I am a nestling eastern phoebe
perched upon the edge
of the moss-lined mud cup
that is the only home I've ever known.

Here, under the roof eves
of the tattered house,
sixteen days have passed
since my egg-tooth
sliced open a world of possibility.

I have grown large in my dreaming
and this womb-bowl too small –

Feted on juicy vain insects,
my plump pin-feathered siblings
and I hunger for
more.

The sky is large and come-hither blue.

I know nothing of the experience
of flight,
but it consumes my definition
of self in entirety.

The distance between here
and the nearest tree is great.

The distance between here
and the rock-hard ground is great.

There are four cats below.
Three of them have been calculating.

I am on the edge.

I am the embodiment of
irrational optimism.

🕊

And I am flying.

Lady Toad

Lady toad,
the color of Virginia red clay,
Buddha-squats in my driveway silently
inviting the sun spent rain
coalescing in ever greater
stream flows
to rush under her pinking pelvic patch
and quench her newly emerged thirst.

I adore and admire her –
perfectly suited to expose herself
to these passionate elements
for long nights of meditative solitude
intermingled with moonlit love making
amidst equisetum stalks at pond edge.

Did my soul long to inhabit her form
but incarnate in the consolation prize?

Nectar

Sixty minutes awake in
the meadow
reveals the Nature of things
someday pronounced discoveries
by those who have been
sleeping all the while.

When was the last time you
relished a sip of honeysuckle –
Really let the clear beads of nectar
languish on your taste buds
instructionally?

How many blues do you
know of the sky that has been
your companion
since birth?

The male cardinal, the wine berries,
and the box turtle's eye
are cadmium red,
alizarin crimson,
and lust.

How glorious to know a sedge
from a grass
and to fervently listen
to their stories
for sixty minutes

As the goats forage.

Simply Divine

I am tempted to find ways
to say that "I love you,"
but Nature has already
said them all.

Let us then surrender,
all together,
to the bright beaches
and the rugged mountain tops.

Let us lay in leaf beds
and meadows of tender
new grasses courting
delicately budding flowers.

When the fawn skips
through her first puddle
and leaps with delight

and the fox pup catches
its very first snowflake
upon the tip of its soft
muzzle,

know that this is everything
that I want to speak
to you my Beloved.

In this mirror
we are wild
and everything tangible
is a brush stroke
of the invisible hand
that tells us
over and over again,

We are human,

And this embodiment
is simply divine.

Storm Clouds

I've been watching these big black clouds
roll in and roll by.

"Storms coming," they say.

The common gray treefrogs concur,
trilling their liquid welcome
to the opulent gods of thunder and lightening.

A tall pine might singe and smolder,
but in the largest puddle there will be amplexus
and whatever ecstasy frogs know.

Ancient ceremonies linger all around us
keeping the Earth turning on her axis.

The choreography takes you
into consideration.

Why don't you dance?

❧

Yesterday the cold spring rains pouring
off the front lip
of Thor's double-headed hammer
caught me on the crest
of Lydia Mountain.

We walked miles together,
each asking questions of the other:

"Can I trust your touch against my skin?"

"Yes," I replied.

Tadpoles In Tire Rut

Five hundred eighty seven
American toad tadpoles
Anaxyrus americanus,
black as pupils,
swim the shallows
of a tire rut.

Not a single limb bud
promises an impending hop.

The Sun knows this.

I imagine many would scoff
at the foolishness
of the two pudgy, wart-covered
night lovers who swooned
and spawned here
under a naked Moon.

Me?

No. Not me.

I kneel, a student.

Only true masters
have the capacity to
put such faith
in the ephemeral.

The Beloved's Breath

If you have suffered long enough
to know your heart and soul,
a moment will arrive
in which you realize—

The breath that you have been
exchanging with the Universe
is that of your Beloved.

From this moment onward,
insist that the Past
and the Future,
bow in utmost respect
of the Present.

The Fiddlehead Song

The voice rose like musty fragrance,
from leaf-littered substrate to my ear.

"Do you love me?"

I stooped low.

"Do you love me?"
inquired harlequin green fern
in fiddlehead curl and tuck.

"Of course I do,"
I replied.

"Then, please sing me a song."

I balked.

Here the delicate melodings of thrushes
disarm choirs of angels
hand-selected by the gods.

I could offer nothing better than an
off-pitched Corvid grok.
On a good day.

"I can gift you some water,
or how about my favorite ring?"

I was hopeful.

"Sing me a song."
My hopes were dashed.

So I sat there at trailside for 36 straight hours,
nervously relocating last Autumn's acorns among piles.

How to honor, not insult?

I mused and agonized
as sunlight and moonlight
took turns wandering through the nascent woods.

And then a cool breeze stirred
the understory and me.

"It's all about intent,"
came the re-minder from my
exasperated mystic pal
on a higher mountain far away.

"Intento!"

Indeed.

I sighed and giggled at
my human folly.

And then I claimed
who I am.

Fire ignited deep within my belly cauldron,
causing feisty cleansing steams
to rise within
and purify.

Dews burning off at dawn
serve the forest similarly,
perhaps.

And so, with great intent, I sang:

"I love you…"

to the harlequin fiddlehead,

alas,

my voice every bit as
unabashedly wretched as I'd feared.

Alas.

But before I could offer up an apology
worthy of such outlandish disgrace,

the *Osmundia* fern replied:

"That's the most beautiful
thing I've ever heard,"

and unfurled.

The Indigo Bunting

Listen now
to the perfumed voice of
the indigo bunting's
"sweet, sweetie, sweet."

How can all of Summer
fit itself into so
tiny a bird?

Here now is Dusk
to silence
the gent.

Oh, spare your tears
my Inner Beloved –

Do not forlorn.

At the first kiss of Dawn
his love notes
will find us.

Why else would we Awaken?

The Unfurling

I cannot help but be moved
by the silent unfurling
of fiddlehead and
floral opulence.

What if I could come undone
with such beauty
and willful surrender?

Grace is the heart throb of the Beloved.

Let me speak with a tongue
of liquid pearls
and repeatedly turn mySelf
inside out
until my heart is evident to even
the weariest eye.

This, I feel,
is what it means
to unfold –
to risk to blossom
amidst a world of witnesses.

The Vittles Of Death

The broad-winged hawk
raised from the rocky creek bed
with a time-limited garter snake
in her talons.

I knew the bird by the
horizontal white tail barring
and the rapid flap of wing
as she rose toward the emerging canopy veil.

I knew the snake by the
vertical yellow stripes
running the length of body to tail.

They gleamed in the sunlight
stored up by the poplar leaves
for cloudy days
such as this.

What of him was not twisted
and entwined in a mutual
death grip with scaly hawk feet
streamed downward –

though in mid air,
gravity still laying a claim
saying,

"You will return to me."

Perhaps all of us knew gravity
wasn't expecting to see that snake
again in the same configuration
of embodiment.

Most of us were okay with it,
under the circumstances.

So bird and snake got me thinking
about how we living beings
must feed our inner beloved
on the vittles of Death.

Love notes take many forms:

Here my Beloved are the chords of attachment
to beliefs proven too small and inflexible,
to things that constrict and clutter,
and to all those who can only embrace us in pathologies of pain.

Here too I lay down all of the possessions
that ego has acquired through the depletion
of Self and Other.

There are many.

Let me nourish you my Dearest,
tending cellular breath and memory,
on the flesh of animal and plant.
Though I'd like to promise you that every
being came to our lips by choice,
I don't know this to be true.

Our gratitude need be far greater than
Grandmother's mourning.

I kept walking,
knowing somewhere beyond my sight
the extended arm of a large tree on mountain slope
was hosting hawk and serpent
at the shared breakfast table of Gain and Loss.

But before this story was completely over,
I came upon another common garter snake –
this one warming belly in the middle of a winding gravel road.

His tongue flicked in and out,
tasting, sensing.

I said,

"Hello Love,"

and gently moved him out of harm's way.

Summer

Affections

This is what you can learn from a bee:

Do not be stingy with
your affections for the flowers
that surround you.

An abundance of beauty
to be delicately visited upon
is no curse.

Open your heart to the possibility
that the Beloved has
chosen your form
through which to make
love with all of Life.

Answers For Mary

Yes!
I saw it, its bill like the compass needle
which is wholly committed to truth.
I knew of its pertinence the very moment
my heart took flight.
You see, beauty isn't for figuring.
Beauty exists only for the embodiment of beauty —
a holy union of form and essence
to be lived into the world like
the sacred contract between mated swans.
And oh yes,
with this,
I've changed my life.

Note: This poem is a response to questions asked by Mary Oliver in her poem, *The Swan*.

Berry Picking

Right arm outstretched.
Thumb and forefinger
poised for delicate
pluck.

Memory and anticipation
rise and spiral
like two strands of DNA
in a rambunctious act of creation.

Herbaceous nibbles,
red and robust,
are offered in abundance
at the sky-cast perk
of bramble tangle

not by accident.

Summer's succulence
is juicy bait for the soul.

Court it,

And eventually you'll learn
that every thorn in life
is an invitation to
slow down
and be attentive.

It's the only way
to harvest fruits.

Cicadas

The curanderos have shed
their last underworldly skin
and taken to the trees.

Chakapa wings drone icaros,
incanting me into my
animal nature
and beyond all hope
of aloneness.

Since my very first summer,
this has been
what a million essential insects
have asked of me.

Today I heard them.

꧂

When I was a young girl
I'd pluck cicada exoskeletons
off tree trunks and fence posts.

Bronze and sun-crisped,
I'd delight in the concept that
form can be outgrown.

I adorned my ear lobes with them,
and my fingers —
Like priceless jewels,
the riches of the wooed and betrothed.

Little then did I know
that it was this child's play
that would teach me
how to fall in love.

⚘

I said, "Yes!"
and became a bride
to the world.

Co-Dependency

If only the thunder
kept to its promise,
we'd have rain.

Sometimes even the sky
knows longing –

Feels an inability to meet
and be met at the humid
interface of Earth and Cosmos.

The old dogwood tree
hasn't known the elements
to be so spare in their
courting,

and its leaves droop,
as if sorrowed.

There went a dragonfly
who cannot find
a pond.

The hummingbird races
against time as the
pink phlox
desiccate.

Whoever classified
co-dependency as a
pathology,

Was never in love
with Life.

Hermit Thrushes In The Morning

On an overcast morning in July,
hermit thrushes
ping-pong snippets of their
liquid melody between
north and south ridges.

I don't understand
the loquacious banter
and I think this tragic.

If a pair of angels stood
in my midst,
would I just carry on,
neglecting to surrender my being
to the symphony of their
holy language?

Intimacy is the turnkey to the soul.

Unbearable passion is what births
everyday miracles.

Why choose to explain a cloud
rather than lie on your back
in tall grasses
and watch a menagerie
shapeshift as it passes?

I don't claim to have any answers,

But I know this world wasn't made
to entertain the diminutive thoughts
of reasonable people.

This world was made for those
whose heart breaks
for want of a grand romance
in which they can
never fully partake.

Sliver Moon

Sliver Moon awakens me at 4:00am.

"What is it?" I ask.

She says, "Rise."

That's all, just "rise."

I walk out the door and into the stickiness of night.

She's in the East,
reclining on the horizon line,
skinny, even waif-like.

You can tell that she has the capacity
for voluptuousness,
a saucy fullness,
but she's not embodying it,
not now,
not at this moment.

But, how she illuminates!

This fascinates me.

I could walk the mountain trails
without so much as a stumble
for the guidance she provides,

Yet so little of her is visibly present.

She has a good laugh
at my bewilderment,
remarking with an erudite chortle:

"As long as I claim
everything in Shadow,"
she says, "I am whole."

Huh.

And I claim the Sacred Fool of me,
with a giggle.

Suddenly, I'm brighter.

Summer Rain

You came like a long absent lover
at the end of a parched day,

gentle at first –

Fully present, I thought,
this will last the night.

Oh Welcome!

But then,

Such fervor!

I wondered in that moment if
it was our desperately
wanting you
that had unbridled your thunderous passions.

It seemed as if even you longed
to surrender to the Other's
most deeply sculpted longing.

But then,

How could you?
So soon you departed!

We are left feeling unquenched.

Do you hear?

Lips merely brushing past each other
can say nothing
of a kiss.

The Breeze

What is the breeze other than

children's laughter,
last breaths,
and lover's kisses blown
as hopes and despairs
in the same desirous language
the world over?

Wing beats of butterfly and bird,
and the angel you refuse to acknowledge,
all trying to nudge
the Wanderer of you
into the vacant arms of The Great Mystery.

Leaf slides against leaf
like a bow rides a string during
the third course of
instrumental love making.

"Shhhhh," they say to every other name
but the one that has been
trying to reach your parched lips
since the moment of your
well-intended conception.

It could all begin with
the nerve endings
in your skin.

When will you stop ignoring
that which touches you?

The Cattail

"I thought that I had told you
about joy," said the cattail…

Toes wiggling in the soft
marsh muck,

Practiced hips swaying
in the breeze,

Undressing silky seed tufts
with a pleasurable sigh
and impish grin.

"Were you not listening?"

The Insistent Moth

Why do you insist
on the long beaten path
of suffering, and
sacrificing your glory-winged being
to the light?

You are of no service
crumpled under a lamp shade
or singed at candle toe.

Do you not know that
there is a lucid holiness
to be had in
the dark abyss?

Reject not the black heavens.

You have caterpillared
and cocooned.
Though death to form
may seem like a way of life,

This time the stars are
counciling you
to Live.

Oh my love,
what would it take
to extend your heart
and flutter your soul
while in the cup of
my gentle hands?

Out the door.

I have faith —

When no longer an addict
of self-flagellation,

The Light that craves You
will enlighten within.

The Nightingale

The nightingale presses her
soft feathered breast
into the spike of the thorn,

penetrating her own aching heart
as her song dies
at sunset.

Or does she?

What if, instead,

The nightingale melods her
melancholy into the world's
most lovely verse,

so strong and convincing
in the depth of its sincerity
that the rose sheds its thorns
into the previous season's
leaf litter and raises its
most fragrant blossomed branch
skyward, as a thrown
for her to perch upon
as she sings her heart outward
at sunset?

Self-inflicted wounds
are an option,

so too is the courage to
feed pain as a holy sacrament
to Truth and Beauty.

Only the latter speaks to Love.

I know birds well enough
to believe the nightingale's
song emerged from swallowing
whole the ancient sorrows
of the wounded feminine,

gestating them around the
turns of the Great Spiral,

and gifting them back to the
world in new-born form.

This is not lost power,

but forgotten power.

Well, not completely forgotten.

Within you there is a nightingale
and there is a rose bush,

you've been referring to them
as all the things that you long
to manifest,

but have been afraid to deserve
because a woman
you respected once showed
you how to lean into thorns

and you believed that's how
it had to be,

always.

This poem is here to say:

"That's not true."

These words are a song that
came to me on the rose-scented
breeze,

one evening,

at sunset,

carried in a voice that my blood knew

as kin.

It was the sound produced across the
lactating vocal chords
of Remembering Woman,

re-membering.

Re-membering to me her primal ties
to the innate courage
to embody Life.

For so many generations we have
been dying away
at our own hands.

It's time to step clear of
the thorns,

isn't it?

You've been sensing this too,

I know.

When Remembering Woman asked
me what she could do to help,

I asked for my own song,

a song likened
to the nightingale's most lovely
sunset song.

I was absolutely sure this would do it.

She said to me,
"You've been singing it
all along, Dear Girl."

"Oh?" I replied.

"Yes," she went on.

"But now you must believe in
what you sing.

That's the difference between
being a girl and being a woman.

The girl knows the words.

The woman knows within her
what they mean."

And, so, at sunrise,
that's the choice I made,

to admit that I know what my
own song means.

The rose bush blushed when
it heard me say it outloud.

I figure that's a very good
place to start.

The Primary Drought

The water lilies
can't explain
why they lie in a crispy heap
on a bed of crackled red clay,

or where the frogs
have gone.

It's early in the season.

But, when the rain stops
a silence sets in.

Those who have not
yet given up their bodies,
pray that Death is so otherwise
occupied that he doesn't notice
they still swill the firebrand air.

I walk through tinder fields
of tall chicory,
blue flowers closed off
to a nauseous sun.

Interesting isn't it,
how so many people
stop to talk about
the drought?

"Tragic," they say.

And I wonder about hearts
folded
up tight against the light

and what it would take to saturate
the human spirit with a love
for this world.

Could our full presence
float flowers?

I'm open to the possibility.

Fear is a stingy master though,
and we in-habit the primary drought,
I think.

The torment of this craving landscape
is a merciless repercussion.

"Tragic," I say.

To Be Moved

Finally I have meditated
long enough
to realize
stillness is a ruse.

Everything riding this
rotund blue dervish
is in constant motion.

What the honeysuckle-infused breeze
asks of us
is not contemplative passivity,

But an active surrender to the possibility
of being moved.

What Is Joy To The Snapping Turtle?

What is joy to the snapping turtle?

His beaky jowl open wide
does not invite a kiss.

His algae-slimed carapace
is rough around the edges,
sculpted by millennia of quarrels
with the world.

It does not invoke cuddle, or caress.

Dare you seek his intimate company,
he will hiss, puff, and rise.
Insist, and be met by a strike
of serpentine appearance and precision.

He has no patience for your curiosity,

No want for admiration or allegiance.

Coo and he will think you ridiculous.

When on land,
he has no retreat from your love
and it scares him.

But oh give him the substrate of
pond bottom muck
and all that he has learned
of passion comes alive.

Like a monk who knows
a specific mist-enshrouded mountain
as the extension
of his soul,

the snapping turtle glides
along a thoroughfare of beaver channels
and snacks on lizard's tail plants
as a matter of meditation

and transpersonal expression.

Watch this ancient master long enough
and you will discover what joy is.

Joy is surrendering your entire being
to the element to which you belong.

When They Make Love

The Sun comes each day to
court the Earth,
warming her body with his
radiant heart.

She blushes streams
and ponds and rivers
when he woos.

And when they make love,
mists arise.

Wild Honey

True Masters will fall to their knees
in fits of reverent weeping
to discover a hive
of wild honey.

How such a tiny insect can fill
a deeply wounded heart
with a golden viscous syrup
so sweet
so nourishing…

Reach inside.

This must be the meaning
of Life.

Autumn

A Walking Stick Sighting

I met a six-legged walking stick today,
an ochre apparition on late summer
redbud twig.

We sat and talked as the sun
chased its tail in the time-short leaves.

I asked him what he knew about
courting the Beloved.

Without hesitation or bewilderment,
this tiny Master of optical disillusion
replied:

"The eyes don't register
what the heart can't see."

Asters Under A Hunter's Moon

In bold defiance of nothing
we convene under the Hunter's Moon,
white asters blooming
thighs to ankles,
a wedding train
that spans the width of this trail
and down the Path
eternally.

Life proposed at conception,

but it has taken me
decades to yield to
my worthiness as a blushing bride.

The owl says, "Who?"

And I declare, "me" —

Committing to an inextricable partnership
with the World
at the altar
of a humble and privileged
embodiment.

This breath says, "Yes."

And so does this one.

Autumnal Equinox

When the rain
falling softly
on goldenrod blooms
streams from my own eyes
as tears of gratitude for
an abundant harvest of wisdom,
I know that I have
lived another season.

May the breath of my Beloved
reach for me in the days ahead,
cool and deliberate,
loosening my leaves
and setting them to fly
in spirals of decay
and communion.

Naked I entered the world,
and naked I will come again
into the darkness.

Only my barren secret
is a shroud.

Shush with your whisperings!

It is true. Yes!

Even in times of scarcity,
I lie with the Beloved at my side
and feel a warmth
and wealth
that this age knows simply as
Belonging.

Cellular Memory

I wrote you a poem
last night
upon a shard
of memory.

These tiny cells of mine
resonate with the primordial
whisperings of
kindred dust.

Every part of me
has been something else
that embodied
passion.

The veins of this crimson maple leaf
may share an identity
with a past or future
lover.

"Tangible intimacy with the world,"

says the tree who
witnesses my rebirths,

"begins with gratitude
for the forgotten lives
that give you life."

Each Sunrise

I fell in love with you
the moment
you brushed my cheek with
Dawn's waning starlight.

Never before have I been
gifted this morning serenade
by these formless crickets –
all beautifully singing to their death
at the hand of the first frost.

Nor have I ever been greeted
at the threshold of home and Home
by these three Sufi crows
and this flock of Zen chickadees
all reminding me that self-expression
is a righteous act of courting
the air we breathe.

The witch hazel leaves are damp
with raindrops that lived only
to take their place
in the soil at my feet
an hour ago.

Today, this Day,
you are my
Beloved.

May there be noted in whatever
part of me is eternal
a re-minder that the
Faithful meet with open hearts
each sunrise.

Falling From Grace

Where I sat on the crumbling brick wall
the pigeon fell,
gasping its last two breaths in my lap
while our eyes introduced our souls.

When I looked to heavens above,
there was only sky, cobalt blue.

What were the chances?

I know what it is to fall from grace –

That rocket-shot tumble
facilitated by your own dead weight
thundering the surface identity into
a direct collision course with
the very foundation of Life.

The impact is the point.

So many times, I've missed it.

Sigh.

It took a poisoned pigeon
to teach me this:

"Rest your weary wings
and unfold your heart
on the way down."

It's the only way
to land with Grace.

Fallow

Plowed and harrowed,
but left unseeded.

What an odd and exhausting
period of rejuvenation
this is.

The dark rich soil of me longs
to support new growth,
to feed Life-sustaining nourishment
to a soul-starved world.

Oh please,

Tell me what nutrients
I still need claim
to be deemed worthy of seed.

Kernels of hope fly past
in crow beaks
but there is never an
effort made to plant.

Rain comes,
and the Sun shines
deliciously upon my hungry body
but I have nothing
to bequest in reciprocity.

So deeply rooted
are my woes
amidst this positively-intended
abandonment.

I wonder in the dark hours,

Is it the chemistry of tears
you seek?

And I offer electrolyte salts
in streams.

Still I remain fallow.

❧

Hafiz tells me
a divine seed, the crown of destiny,
is hidden and sown on an ancient, fertile plain
that I hold the title to.

How then does one reveal the
fore-ordained Gift of Self?

Dowsing with willow brings
me to the core:

Embryo and endosperm.

In essence, it is me
feeding the offering
of sustenance that
is myself.

I am entitled to give.

These sweet tears of joy
 I absorb,
and swell.

And swell.

So this is what it feels like
to break free
from the hardness
and rise!

In The Dark Of Night

In the dark of night,
between the Sun's abandonment
and the Moon's possession,
there can be a great temptation
to run.

Don't.

Sit. Be still.

Invite the Beloved to haunt
every aspect of
your vulnerable being.

What's the sense of being truly alive
if you won't commit to being ravished
by the exquisite tenderness of
of the unseen?

The breeze picks up and takes your skin
into the pucker of its lips.

This is merely foreplay.

Pruning

Can you live with the scent
of larkspur on your lips
while others seek to destroy you
because of memories
they can't recall?

Truth is not found on the
material plane.
It resides in the imprints
you've left during your
comings and goings
on the Other Side.

Don't let yourself be hooked
into playing a role you
died to lifetimes ago.

The Beloved never manifests
a single rose.
You too must choose to
be a bloom a hundred times over.
Let the thorns be protectors
not villains.

And even if the shears do come,
bless your courage
for having shown up in this life
well enough
to be noticed.

Taking A Walk

The turkey vulture's rocking,
dihedral shadow crosses over me,
the road, the meadow, the mountains,
and a future
that can only be scripted
by those aspects of me
apprenticed to longing.

My feet proceed:
One, two, three four.
One, two, three, four,
Like someone has told them
that what is at the end of this
journey is so
worth the
effort.

Upon my approach,
a pair of brown thrashers rise
from the their dust bath
cup,
emptying the Earth body
of their bodies.

I kneel and finger the
lingering warmth.
Do they know that I look
upon their effort to rid
themselves of parasites
as a hand gesture of
the Beloved?

This is what it is all about,
isn't it?

How we choose to See things.

The Directions Of The Geese

Between the clouds
and the Great Mystery,
forgotten by all but our
most primal being,
lies an atmosphere
where we can meet those
we've denied and abandoned.

Soul fragments linger
in the ethers
awaiting recognition
and a mustering of courage.

They count the seasons
of their exile by
the directions of the geese.

Won't you call
yourSelf
Home?

The Mud Puddle

Like a magenta sunrise,
this passing moment
can linger a lifetime
without a promise.

Gratitude is the indefinite host
of the Beloved's caress,
if even brief,
delicate,
surprising.

There is nothing shallow
about waters that
quench the thirst of a longing soul.

Splash barefoot
in that mud puddle,
wholeheartedly.

It is what remains of a brief
interlude between
Heaven and Earth.

In the hours left before
this sunset,
there is ample time
to count everything that
touches you
as a blessing.

The Silence

Those who say...

"There is silence in the forest."

"There is silence at the lake."

"There is silence throughout the desert."

"There is silence as the bluefish schools
the surface of the tourmaline ocean."

"There is silence as the barn owl hovers
above vole-cowering meadow."

"There is silence as the honey bee ambles
across coneflower head under cloud-wisp sky."

...Have never heard their own voice

offering up the prayer of gratitude

that the silence

was created for.

Touching

The sun broke
through the rain clouds
the very instant
the cormorant rose and rippled
Autumn-colored
waters.

I'm sure they kissed.

What is this that I have witnessed?

When the spirits borrow
the fleeting body
dreams become tangible
possibilities.

A hand can reach into
another
to comfort and inspire
the Soul.

Winter

An Answer

At the end of every day
there is a silence that creeps
in.

It's the unoccupied space
filled with memories
and what ifs.

Sometimes it has a name.

Usually not.

It keeps me in good company,
dependable
and never argumentative.

We've started growing old
together,
like long familiars do.

But lately my gratitude for
such a simple departure
into the night has begun
to wane.

I hear voices after the sun
sets.

One of them sounds like mine.

I dare myself to believe
in the other,

with little success
as of yet.

What does one do with
an interlude
in which a single candle
burns

faster than the red wine?

Perhaps this is a space
reserved for prayers.

If so, I am lacking,

for I have forgotten
for that which I used to pray
so heartedly.

"Maybe," says the flickering
flame,

"you are not to pray,

but to become the answer

to a prayer."

Courting The Darkness

I am sure that it is
the darkness that
shows us how to find
the light.

I have been with Darkness
long enough
to have come to know
its tenderness –

to feel its hand deliciously
upon the small of my
back,

leading.

Someday this dance
will be revealed,

but not too soon,
I hope.

My Beloved wanders at
the edge of moon beams
and courts me in the hip-loose
swaying of long afternoon
shadows.

Only when I am standing
in my own light
can I see Him,

and everything looks
beautiful from
here.

Departing Storms

I have opened all of my
doors to the oncoming
winter storm.

The wind howls lullabies
and the branches of the naked
sycamore flail
as it dances,
entranced to music
that I have long ago forgotten
how to drum up.

Dark grey clouds come
to me across the western ridge,
running southward
and then East.

My eyes follow their
intent to be somewhere
soon.

Should this be my prayer today?

This cleansing of my
inner landscape with your
mood of intolerance to
settled things?

Too much of me has settled, perhaps.

Settled for circumstances
smaller than I deserve,
for conveniences,

for momentary supplications
that rendered the next moment
without advent of utility
to the soul.

It's interesting, really,
how much this life of mine
seems to need of your
surging body.

Somewhere along the way
I think we must have taken
each other as tempestuous
lovers
and I've failed to remember
it until now.

So maybe this will be my
prayer today:

That you open to receive me
in your throttling arms
as I take to the mountain crest,
offering to catch your tears
in my mouth and call out
the salty om that will most certainly
bring us together
in a familiar grip of longing.

But, no, I think not.

Today, today I want to
pray as the raven prays,
catapulting myself on the drama
manifest of your thermals
and gliding off to meet with
turquoise blue.

Today my prayer is for the
courage to leave
all the storms that no longer
serve me as stunned
wisps memorizing the
curvature of my back
as I depart.

The ancient bones of me have
rested long enough to have
learned the cadence of
tranquility.

This is the earth song that I
want to recall when the
winds gust within.

In The Frost Crystals

I've been watching for
signs of your breath
in the frost crystals
on my morning window pane.

When the sun embodies
her robust bosom,
they melt
and so do I,

letting longing be my
own personal
burning.

The narcotic pain
of weeping
singes my
very soul.

Surely you know nothing
of this.

And, that is why I
don't give up
this courtship
easily.

In the unrequited affair
with the wild,
with the invisible,
with the intangible

there exists the opportunity
to build the capacity
for unconditional love.

In This Way

The pudgy voles must be
nestled deeper now,
the meadow grasses damp
with the weeping of
half-hearted snow flurries,

And the fox and owl
tucked in by morning light,
stomachs robust and satiated
or burning with a hunger
strong enough to feed fear
into the hours ahead.

This is how I awaken.

Life on earth is a written language
that is read through the
living of it.

What is most tempting of
this day is everything that
I don't know about its
unfolding.

My Beloved is like this,
fully present yet always
out of reach of anything
intent on the possession
of answers that would shorten
the moment's extended hand.

To be betrothed to
the Great Mystery
is to say "yes" to everything
that cannot be planned:

The next breath,

The next lover,

Death,

And how each will
take you in their arms,

with, or without,
mercy.

The vole knows only the
last pinch of the talon,
and the tongue-pressing
swallow of the fox,

but even in this,
there is time enough to
breathe out these words,

"So that was my life.

I am so very grateful."
And in passing this way,
so many times,
you place your own
punctuation marks
in the Great Story,
Stops,
starts,
and the kind of exclamations

that can only come
from embodied feeling.

In this way,

You live and die,

in the way all
exhausted
lovers do.

Solstice Moon

She is there,
moved to western sky
round and red and full
like an areola at birthing
time.

I, on my front stoop,
am riding the planet
that casts Her into shadow.

Some would say,
"for but a short while."
Yet, it feels like the
time has been so very long,
so very long,
already.

I hear the drumming of ancients
in the meadow
by the wood.

Is it a beat of survival fears
or celestial celebration?

I check inside.

Both.

Memories arise
of the annihilations
we have witnessed.

I know where to find
the doorway
to Lemuria.

Memories arise
of the passionate love we
have made with
our heavenly bodies.

The burning bite of the
enthusiastic Sun
is of no comparison
to the patient, delicate
kisses of the stars.

Here now,
I am witness as She
surrenders –
taken and released
by Darkness.

And I love Her
in afterglow
so strong it sets
the snow alight.

As the pinking fingers
make their way,
I wonder
if in this new radiant
light
of dawn

even the Creator
will discover something
never before seen.

Sacraments

How does last night's fallen snow
feel about the morning sun's radiant touch?

Is there a deep yearning to be melted,
or is there a great fear of death?

I whisper:

"They can be one, the same."

The sharp-shinned hawk throws himself,
like Cupid's hell-bent arrow,
head on into the bough-damp cedars.

He has faith in a universal memory
that has never occupied him personally.

"There will be nourishment at the core of
this dark and tangled thicket."

And he is correct,

Emerging with brown, floppy-necked sparrow
in his blood-warmed talons.

He makes no apology for taking a life
to secure his own,
But he does pull each of the sparrow's feathers
and set them fluttering free into the blue of sky
as his particular way
of making an offering to the Holy.

And is this what it's all about? I wonder:

Every act of life, a sacrament.

The Humming

I'm learning that there are bonds
of holy union
that cannot be undone
by mere mortals.

Swans know of them,
and dogs,
and children under the age of five.

And every other being on this planet.

When did we stop regarding
every breath as sacred,

and every eye we look into
and every hand that brushes against
ours?

I saw the filaments dancing today,
the ones that criss-cross lifetimes
and geographies.

They were humming a tune that I
have heard before in the natal waters.

It has only one note.

That's all it needs.

When you remember it,
you remember me.

When I remember it,
I remember you.

It's really quite amazing that we have lost
our way…

Really, it is.

The hummingbird has been trying to remind
us of our origin
while we take pity on it for the lack
of a song.

Oh my Beloved:

How I have forsaken you
in the austerity of these hurried times.

Were it not for the touch of sunlight
on a cold winter's day,
I might have forgotten the endlessness
of your reach.

Always the bindings that unite us are there,
across them flowing an abundance of Grace
and urging.

Longing is the form of that urging.

It is no vapid pain,
but a life blood of sentiment
through which the Holy
feeds us on dreams.

It is the umbilicus of Love,

and when it is cut,

I've come to learn,

something dies.

In the story of every fallen god
and every unlived life
there is this Truth,

and a deafening silence.

The Melting Point

Can you be present long enough
to watch the frost
melt in the hand
of the morning sun?

Solid becomes liquid,
puddles,
and drops one wet rainbow pearl
at a time onto the
mossy tongue of the Earth.

And she laps,

with a twinkle in her eye.

I'm wondering:

Have you ever let anyone
warm you long enough
to know,
with all certainty,
that you've found your
melting point?

A sunset might move you.

Maybe a white jasmine flower,

or its scent on the breeze.
Perhaps a wobble-legged foal
standing for the first time
can cause your heart
to risk and fall.

But, have you let another
of your own kind melt you —

to turn your heart
into a thousand shimmering
tears wept in ecstatic gratitude
for the arrival of that moment
in which you finally have no
doubt, you are alive?

I ask this because I See
that so many of us have
forgotten, and been
forgotten.

Brigid's well needs
water;

the fish can grant
no answers to your
prayers without it.

There is an alchemy that
we must live into this
world if we want
change.

If I can't melt you,
and you can't melt me,

what is the point?

The water of life
am I,
and are you,
and we are all
so very thirsty.

So let us do this:

Let us see each Other
as beauteous forces
of Nature.

Let us agree to touch
each Other,

and be vulnerable
to being changed
by the Other's touch.

Let us yield to the
perpetual flow of
essential love,
nurturing what grows.

Let us commit to making
our own melting point
humanity's
Great Turning point.

The Silent Retreat

Sometimes you have to go
into your thick quietude
alone

Because no one
can meet the curve
of your words.

Seven billion people
and still so much
empty space
at our sides.

Winter is for teaching
about these things:

The sap draws down.

The herbal layer dies away,
making a place
for nothingness.

The cardinal
speaks only through
internal dialogue.

Snow can fill the
tracks of a deer in
moments
and only the
snow knows the
story that it has hidden
from the closed eyes
of the world.

This is a silent retreat.

Go then, this way…

Far within the bear's den
where you will
hear your beating heart
echoing in all five chambers.

Speak nothing of the Beloved

until the Beloved has
your name.

Then, you'll know,
emergence
is the only possibility.

The Universe Unfolds

The Universe unfolds,
ever so briefly,
in my arms and
upon my lips.

What magic this is seeks
no logic beyond
the heart's logic,

no promise greater
than the soul's
recollection of
belonging.

How is it that a retreating sun
knows so much about tomorrow's
intangible quest for
today's company?

"My setting is an illusion,"
it says,

"as is separation between
beauty's co-creative
forces."

So, this is timelessly beautiful to me,
like the coo of a turtle dove
reaching an old man's
sentimental ear.

What melts in the winter,
softens the ground
for that which emerges

through the utility of
its own yearning come
spring.

Let the throat choke with
gratitude for the Beloved,

the eyes can say it
all when they drop
tears upon the rose petal
trails that guide the way
to a familiar

Home.

The Winter Wren

How can a little brown bird flit
across your path,
yet remain perched as a precious haunt
in your psyche for days?

The winter wren is a secret
come out from the thick greenbrier
to look you in the eye
and let you know only
that it has suddenly revealed
itself in the brisk, dancing
air.

What secret?

This bird took no measure
to say.

How often aspects of us
show up without announcement
or explanation,

flitting into our awareness
with the hope that we will
See.

We are more mystery to
ourselves than we know.

The sky can't decide
on blue or gray,
and the clouds are directionally
fickle

as I ponder the winter wren
hop-skipping through
my dense woodland.

"What is it you want of me?"
I ask.

"It's a secret,"
is the only reply.

And this is what I concluded:

I can love what I do not know.

Countless bodies are breathing
in windswept thickets
around me,
and without me knowing of them,
or them of me,
we are entwined and my heart holds
inexplicable space for them.

What is yet unrevealed of me, too,
is lovable.

True Nature

Does a bird choose
a branch that
cannot hold it,
or build a nest too
small for its unhatched dreams?

It's not in its nature.

How often have you given
your heart to people
who cannot tend it,
who do not wish to hold space
for your most intimate silences?

Why is it in our nature?

I've seen how a flower can
make an entrance way
perfect for a bee,

How a frog can finish
the call of another.

What is this emptiness
we pursue
in our attempt to know
more than we are?

Tonight I have no answers.

The winter moon is filling herself
up in my window pane
and we behave like strangers
not intent on introductions.

Only the honey in my tea
parts my lips and cajoles
my tongue to speak
with a sweetness

that has yet to ripen
by my will.

Oh,

But it is of no use,

this holding back.

It's simply in my nature
to love.

What vacancy Rumi knew of
idiot compassion,
I know not either.

Two fools
we are,

courting from bedposts
across the span
of different lifetimes.
But the sentiment is no less
in fortitude

for the absence
of the other.

Branches and flowers
manifest
with no promise
of birds and bees.

And so.

Love.

If it is true.

Whooo

Tonight the barred owls
ask their question upon
the chill of dusk;

one from the tulip poplar grove,
the other at creekside.

"Whooo?"

Is what they want to know.

"Whooo?"

It's a dangerous inquiry.

A warrior's initiation right
if you dare seek the answer.

Do you dare?

Do you dare to know
who you truly are?

Coyotes run the crest of the ridge,
yips and howls
formulating the collective voice
of the pack.

Don't listen to them,

they are tricksters.
This is what I have to say:

If you go searching for the
answer,

you will Die.

And if you don't go searching
for the answer,

you will die.

If you want to Live,

you must go searching
for the answer.

The moon will light the way in the darkness,
but only so much as to allow
you to take one uncertain step
at a time,

often, backwards.

You'll find that what the sun illuminates,
is frequently outsized by its
shadow,

and that the shadow has a life of its own.

You are going to have to
befriend it,
as your fellow journeyman.

Be prepared to leave who you
think you are behind
in the quest for
authenticity.

It's best if you put down the large bundle
of "what no longer serves"
at the trail head.

Do bring your most spectacular heartaches
and your deepest wounds;
these are the trail markers that
will help you stay on course.

And too, have within you
a most
beautiful verse.

You cannot fully understand who you
are until you have courted the
Beloved with such wild abandon,
that you become completely undone.

"Whooo?"

from the top of the tallest pine.

"Whooo?"

from the sycamore at the edge of the meadow.
"Who?"

from the moment you were born,

has been the question

gifted by those who

want you to find your way

Home.

Resolutions

I resolve:

To spend more time
talking with trees;

To speak my Truth
and the Truth of those
who cannot speak
for themselves;

To let Nature set the
rhythm of my days
and nights

and the seasons of
my belonging to
this world;

To laugh with children
and some adults too;

To throw a wayward
starfish back
into the ocean;

To dance to the music
that moves me;

To mend a broken wing,
mine,
or someone else's;

To shine as light in the darkness
and become an ever-truer
friend to my shadows
and demons;

To pick up my paint brushes again
and write songs that
I will never sing;

To learn the constellations
and share nights with friends
under starry skies;

To wear purple more often
and paint my toenails
red,

and start contemplating
how I can become
one of those cool
old women when
the time arrives;

To make love,
honoring the sacred
and enjoying this embodiment;

To smile in pictures,
and smile when there
is no one around to notice
that I am smiling;

To find myself in awe of Life,
every day;

To hike in the rain more often,
splash in puddles,
and listen to streams.

To see gardening as co-creative process
and value the time shared
with the Mother;

To be fully present as I prepare my
meals and as I nourish my body,
savoring each bite;

To be of service in my Work
and play
and to play;

To meditate on abundance
and express gratitude
at least as often as I
breathe;

To forgive as an act of
duty to my soul,
a means of
expanding my heart,

and the laying of a
stepping stone on the
path to a better world;

To build community
and mirror beauty
back to all beings;

To be courageously vulnerable
and hang out with uncertainty
as if we were childhood
friends.

To simply be enough.

And.

To love you,
because I can.

Acknowledgments

A deep bow of honor and appreciation is offered to Jason Kirkey and L. M. Browning of Hiraeth Press for making a place for Sacred Reciprocity and courting the Beloved through impassioned words of their own.

I give thanks for and to several dear friends who have provided enthusiastic support throughout the course of this project: C Andrew Barker, Beth Anne Boardman, Andrea Freeman, Scott Hales, Richard Heilbrunn, Chandali Ishta, Patricia Malia, LaRue Owen, J.K. McDowell, Jacquie Roecker, Jane E. Viera, and Alyce Walker. Your kind words, your editorial input, and your presence...are greatly appreciated.

To Frank Owen, my heart-felt gratitude for being a soul friend, a kindred traveler, and prayer-poet, and for taking the time to put your keen eyes to this entire collection.

Great and humble thanks to Trebbe Johnson, Theodore Richards, and Carla Woody for their generous words of endorsement on the back cover. And thank you too for being conduits for the Beloved.

About the Author

Jamie K. Reaser has a deep fondness for the wild, intimate, and unnameable. She received a BS in Field Biology, with a minor in Studio Art, from the College of William and Mary and her doctorate in Biology from Stanford University. She has worked around the world as a biologist, international policy negotiator, environmental educator, and wilderness rites-of-passage guide. She is also a practitioner and teacher of ecopsychology, nature-based spirituality, and various approaches to expanding human consciousness, as well as a poet, writer, artist, and homesteader-in-progress. Jamie has a passion for bringing people into their hearts, inspiring the heartbeat of community, and, ultimately, empowering people to live with a heart-felt dedication to Mother Earth. Her writing explores themes related to Nature and human nature in this magical, yet challenging, time of the Great Turning. She is the editor of the *Courting the Wild Series,* as well as the author of *Huntley Meadows: A Naturalist's Journal in Verse* and *Note to Self: Poems for Changing the World from the Inside Out.* Jamie is a Fellow of the International League of Conservation Writers. She makes her home in the Blue Ridge Mountains of Virginia. Visit her Talking Waters poetry blog at www.talkingwaters-poetry.blogspot.com, or through Talking Waters on Facebook.

I Wish For Only This

The world doesn't need to know
that I have lived,

Or how many times
I have died.

I do not desire my name
to be spoken of
or repeated in form.

Whatever the elements make
of me is fine.

I wish for only this:

That those I have loved
find themselves,

some day,

crumpled over
in the soil,

raining Her with tears
of ecstatic bliss,

because my soft gaze
softened their hearts.

Hiraeth Press

Hiraeth Press is a publisher with a mission.

Poetry is the language of the Earth — not just poems but the slow flap of a heron's wings across the sky, the lightning of its beak hunting in the shallow water; autumn leaves and the smooth course of water over stones and gravel. These, as much as poems, communicate the being and meaning of things. Our publications are all poetry, whether they are poems or nonfiction, and reflect the ideal that falling in love with the Earth is nothing short of revolutionary and that through our relationship to wild nature we can birth a more enlightened vision of life for the future. We are passionate about poetry as a means of returning the human voice to the polyphonic chorus of the wild.

www.hiraethpress.com